Wiring for Beg

Step by Step Guide on How to Wire a House and Do All Manner of Indoor and Outdoor Wiring Projects, With Easy to Follow Projects

Introduction

Electrical wiring problems do happen now and then, and it can be costly to call in an electrician every time you need repairs or installations done. Taking a bold step to learn how to DIY electrical wiring can save you money.

However, electricity can be hazardous; hence you want to learn how to DIY projects efficiently and safely.

How about outdoor wiring projects; can you also fix them well and safely?

If you are eager to carry out excellent wiring projects using safety precautions, then this is the book for you.

It carefully takes you through the basics of what electrical wiring in your home entails, the safety measures you need to take, and explains step by step the projects you can do as a beginner, both indoors and outdoors.

You might be wondering;

- Will I be able to carry out simple home wiring repairs and installations?

- Will I be able to install outdoor fixtures?

- How safe am I when handling electrical projects?
- Is there any important information I need to know before embarking on any project?
- What general aspects of electrical wiring do I need to know?

Well, in this book, you will find;

- Basic training on DIY projects
- Crucial information that you need to know to help you understand your projects better
- What to do to ensure your safety when handling wiring projects
- General knowledge of electrical wiring in the home
- Tips to make wiring in your house easier

...and much more!

Learning how to DIY electrical wiring repairs and installations will not only save you money but will improve the comfort in your home.

Let's get into it!

PS: I'd like your feedback. If you are happy with this book, please leave a review on Amazon.

Please leave a review for this book on Amazon by visiting the page below:

https://amzn.to/2VMR5qr

Table of Contents

Introduction 2

Chapter 1: Basic Components of Electrical Wiring in your Home 6

Chapter 2: Important Aspects of Electrical Wiring That You Need to Know Before Starting on Your Wiring Projects 22

Chapter 3: Electrical Wiring Safety Codes and Preparation for Both Indoors and Outdoors Wiring 32

    Safety Precautions When Working on a Wiring Project 36

    Planning For Your Projects 38

Chapter 4: Common DIY Indoor Wiring Projects .. 40

Chapter 5: Outdoor Wiring Projects 67

Chapter 6: Tips for Easier Electrical Wiring in Your Home 106

Conclusion 109

Chapter 1: Basic Components of Electrical Wiring in your Home

We constantly depend on electricity. We need it to carry out duties such as cooking, reading, bathing, and washing clothes, to name a few.

When the power goes out because of a storm, tripped breaker, or an electrical fault, you need to understand the basic components of the electrical wiring in your home to help you fix the problem.

Did you know that the utility company is only responsible for the service they offer up to the connection point in your house? After that, the electricity that goes into your house is called the load side, and everything that entails the load side is your obligation. The following are the essential components in your home that you need to understand before learning how to fix anything electrical-related.

1. Electrical Service Connection and Meter

steemit.com

The electric power in your home starts with the electric and power service meter. This is the point at which the service cables of the utility company join to your house. The amount of electricity used in your home is measured by the electrical meter, from which the utility company charges and gives you an electric bill. The meter only runs when electricity is used in your home.

2. Disconnect Switch

bluerooffarms.com

Many homes have a disconnect switch fixed on a wall outside of the house next to the electric meter. This switch is helpful when there's a flash flood or fire or when work needs to be done on the wiring system. When it is shut down, the electric power automatically stops flowing into your home, such that you do not have to enter the house to switch off the power. If your home does not have a separate disconnect switch, then the main circuit breaker in your home's breaker box serves as the disconnect system.

3. Main Service Panel

gettyimages.com

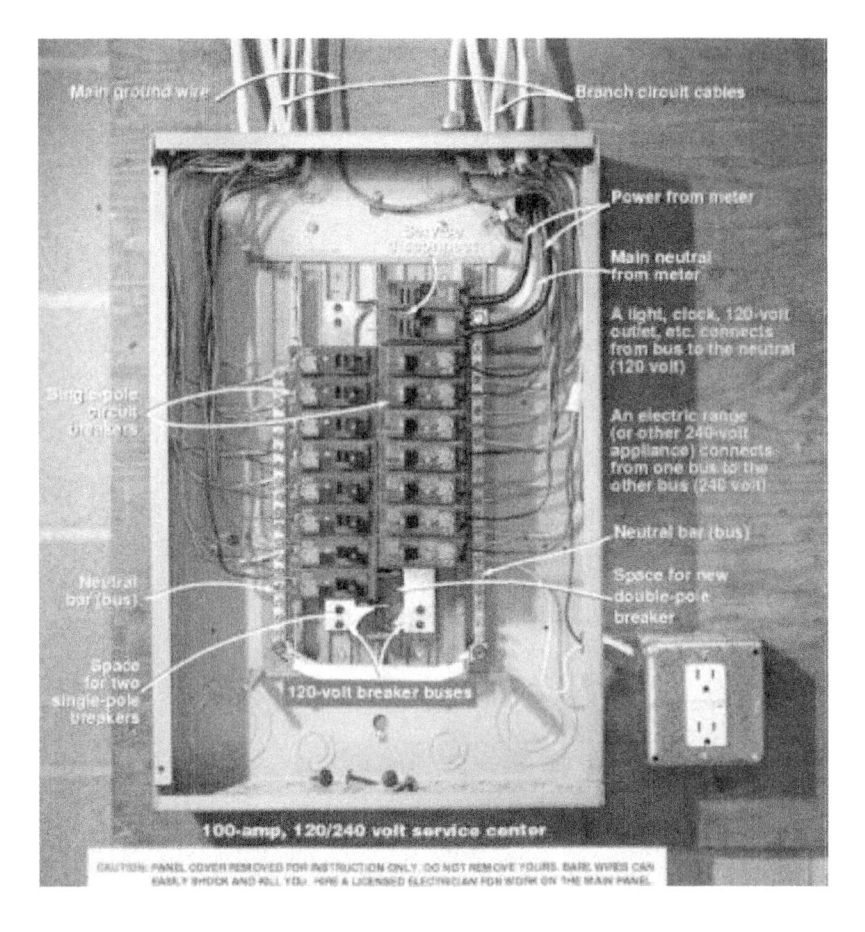

bobvila.com

When electricity is fed into your meter, it is fed into your home's main service panel, known as the breaker box. There are two "hot" large wires connected to big screw terminals inside the box, known as lugs, which provide all the power to the panel.

There's a third cable that is neutral and connects to the neutral bar inside the panel. In other words, electricity is led into the house through the hot wires. It flows through the household electrical system and is returned to the utility via the neutral wire to complete the electrical circuit.

4. The Main Circuit Breaker

thespruce.com

The main circuit breaker is located inside the service panel. The switch controls the electric power to the other circuit breakers inside the box, and it is sized according to the service capacity in your home.

Most homes are provided with 200 amperes. This means that the main breaker carrying 200 amperes can only allow a

11

maximum of 200 amperes to pass through it without tripping. When it is tripped, the current flows to the panel. The main breaker acts as the household disconnect in homes that do not have an external disconnect switch.

Electric power stops flowing to the other circuit breakers in the panel when the main breaker is turned off. However, it is good to note that power is always moving into the panel and to the service lugs, despite the main breaker being shut off, unless the power is shut down from the disconnect switch. There's always a current moving in the electric meter and the utility service lines. It only stops flowing when the utility shuts the power off.

5. The Branch Circuit Breakers

thespruce.com

Below the main breaker inside the panel, you will find branch circuit breakers which control the electric flow to the branch circuits in the house. When you turn off a breaker, the power is shut off from all the appliances and devices connected to that particular circuit. The circuit breaker normally trips on its own if there is a problem, e.g., a fault or an overload in the circuit.

For example, if you are using a high-demand appliance like a heater, toaster, or vacuum, and the power shuts down, then most probably, you have an overloaded circuit. Check if there is a bigger problem by connecting your appliance to another circuit and switching on the breaker. If it trips again when the appliance is not plugged in, you need to call in an electrician. This is an indication that there is indeed a big problem that needs to be fixed, such as a fault.

6. Devices

unsplash.com

Devices are items in the house that use electricity, including appliances, light fixtures, receptacles or outlets, and switches. The devices are connected to the branch circuits, which start from the breakers inside the main service panel.

One circuit can contain multiple devices, fixtures, receptacles, and switches. On the other hand, a single circuit may serve only one receptacle or appliance and is usually used for demanding appliances, such as water heaters, furnaces, and refrigerators. Other appliances like microwaves and dishwashers are normally connected to dedicated circuits, which can be switched off from the service panel without interfering with power flow to other devices. This helps reduce any problems that may occur due to overloaded circuits.

The [National Electrical Code](#) requires a dedicated electrical circuit to serve a single electrical fixture or appliance. The dedicated circuits can serve no other lights, outlets, fixtures, or appliances. They are applicable for use on appliances that have motors to provide enough power for the start-up load to work at peak performance. Dedicated circuits are most convenient for preventing circuit overloads.

7. Switches

istockphoto.com

The devices that turn on and off the lights in your home are called switches. They are available in different colors and styles to suit your design preference. For example, there are dimmer, single-pole, two-way, three-way, or four-way switches.

When the switch is flipped off, it opens the circuit, thereby breaking the circuit and interrupting the power. When you flip on the switch, on the other hand, the circuit closes, and the electric power flows past the switch to the light or to any other device it is connected to.

a) Dimmer Switches

istockphoto.com

Dimmer switches lower or raises the brightness in the electric bulbs. They are normally used in homes or businesses to save energy and to control the lighting. These switches can either be controlled automatically or manually depending on how you have set them.

b) Single-Pole Switch

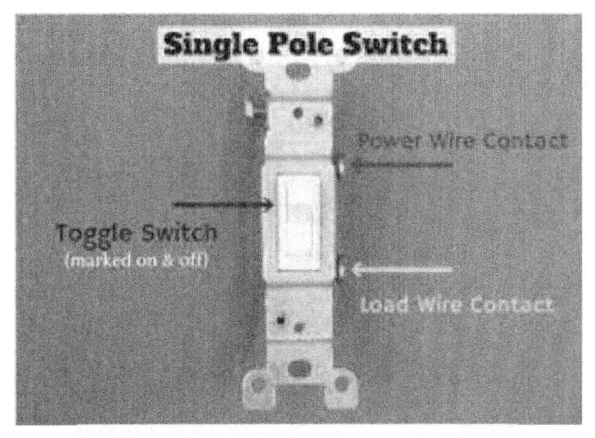

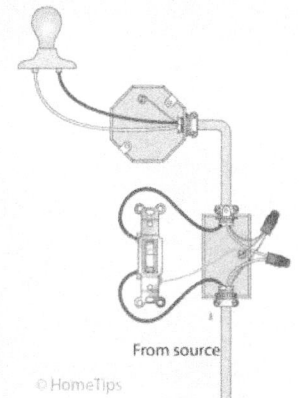

asktheelectricalguy.com

This is the most common and straightforward light switch. When you flip the paddle up, the circuit is completed, turning on the appliances and lights. When the switch is flipped down, the circuit is broken, turning off the lights or appliances. This single-pole switch has two terminals connected to two hot wires, one is the power wire, and the other one is the load wire. The load wire connects to your devices and lights.

A single-pole switch consists of two brass terminal screws found on the side that receive the black or hot wires of the circuit. One black wire originates from the power source, while the other connects to the lights.

When switched off, the power that flows through the black wire interrupts the flow of electricity that connects the fixture to the power source. The black wires are connected to the two main terminals.

c) Two-Way Switch

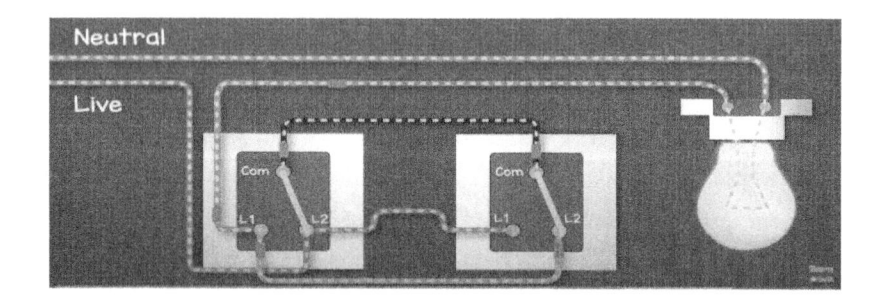

theengineeringmindset.com

The two-way switch can control a light bulb from two different locations. It can be turned off and on from two separate areas; for example, in a stairway where you can switch on the light at the bottom of the stairway and switch it off when you reach the top.

d) Three-Way Switch

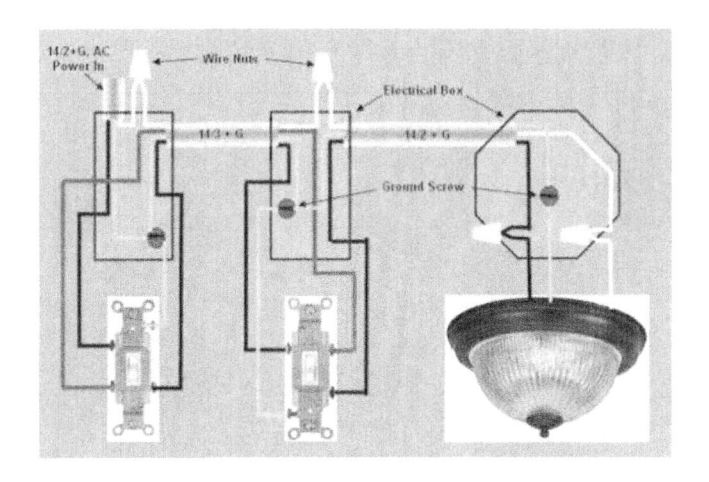

renovation-headquarters.com

A light fixture can be controlled from two different locations using the three-way switch. For example, a three-way switch can be fixed at each end of a stairway or long hallway so that the lights can be turned on from one end and then switched off from the other end. When both toggles are up or down, the circuit becomes complete, and the light fixtures become illuminated. Contrarily the circuit is interrupted when the toggles are in opposite positions and the light fixtures are turned off. Either switch can control the on and off function of the light fixtures at any time.

e) Four-Way Switch

A 4-way switch is achieved by adding an extra switch to an existing 3-way switch circuit. This gives you control of a load from different locations in addition to the two locations that a three-way circuit provides.

8. Outlets

unsplash.com

Electrical outlets or receptacles provide electric power to appliances or plug-in devices. Toasters, vacuums, freezers, lights, televisions, and computers are excellent examples of devices usually plugged into an outlet. The outlets in our homes are normally between 15 amperes to 20 amperes. Outlets specially made for demand appliances such as a clothes dryer may provide between 30 and 50 amperes of power.

Areas in your home, such as the laundry rooms, kitchens, and bathrooms, must have the ground-fault circuit-interrupter (GFCI) protection.

Chapter 2: Important Aspects of Electrical Wiring That You Need to Know Before Starting on Your Wiring Projects.

As a beginner in wiring, you need to understand some aspects of electrical wiring before embarking on your first wiring project. Let's discuss each below:

1. GFCI and AFCI Protection

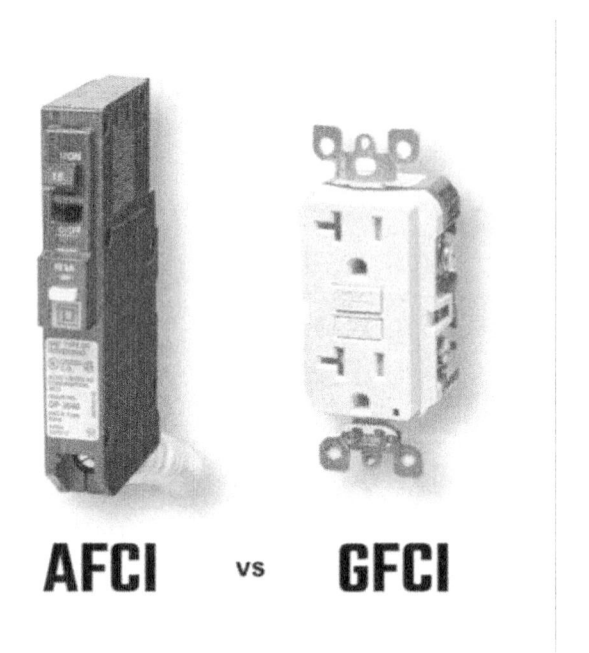

www.dfliq.net

For many years now, Ground Fault Circuit Interrupter (GFCI) has been a requirement for protection purposes. Until recently, the National Electrical Code (NEC) made it a requirement to have another mode of protection, known as Arc Fault Circuit Interrupters (AFCI). By 2002, it became necessary for bedrooms and by 2014, NEC became an obligation to provide AFCI protection in laundry rooms and kitchens. In 2017, it became a prerequisite to have AFCI protection in all living spaces in the home.

a) Ground-Fault Circuit Interrupter Protection (GFCI)

A ground fault happens when a current moves through an unintended path back (current leakage) to an electrical current source when it comes into contact with a grounded surface. For example, a person can become the unintentional path for an electrical current by touching the outer metal part of a toaster oven when it is energized. This is known as an electrical shock, which can be dangerous because it can be fatal.

The GFCI protection comes in handy to protect against electrical shocks in places prone to leakage currents from appliances and power tools. Such locations include places that get moist, including bathrooms, kitchens, and outdoors.

Other places include areas that are likely to have frayed flexible cords or damaged electrical wiring.

How Does a GFCI Work?

The Ground Fault Circuit Interrupter protection is designed to protect you from fatal electrical shocks by de-energizing the electricity within a short time when an electrical current to the ground exceeds certain values. GFCI devices such as receptacle outlets and circuit breakers stop the electric flow from a leakage current to the ground. If the leakage current is approximately 10 milliamps, it's at a dangerous level as it can cause death in 2 seconds when it passes through a person. In a nutshell, GFCI protects against shock to save lives.

Places where GFCI protection is needed include the bathrooms, laundry area, kitchens, shower stalls, and accessory buildings, and garages that have the floor located below or at grade level. It's crucial that you check with NEC for a complete list of areas where FCI protection is necessary.

b) Arc-Fault Circuit-Interrupter Protection (AFCI)

The Arc-Fault Circuit Interrupter Protection (AFCI) protects against arc-faults which can be caused by loose electrical connections and terminals, where flexible cords or electrical wiring have been damaged. For example, a dangerous arcing can occur when the wiring in the wall is pierced by a screw or nail when hanging a picture in the living room.

Other reasons for arc faults include damaged or worn flexible cords and deterioration of cord and cable protective insulation due to excessive heat or sunlight.

How AFCI Works

AFCI devices use advanced technology to monitor the electrical current in a circuit to protect against fire. The technology is designed to detect arcing signatures, which are then de-energized when the electricity reaches dangerous levels.

The technology has been improving with time to the extent that the electrical circuit no longer breaks or trips when it is installed.

Areas Where AFCI Protection is Required

Similar to GFCI devices, AFCI devices need to be installed in locations that can be accessed easily. That means if there is a need for inspection, renewal, or operation, these locations can be reached quickly. For multifamily, two-family, and one-family buildings, areas where AFCI protection is needed are in the bedroom, family room, dining rooms, kitchens, laundry areas, closets, and recreation rooms.

Refer to NEC for a complete compilation of locations where AFCI protection is needed.

2. Types of Wiring, Sizes, and Their Color Codes

You need to understand the sizes, types of wires, and their color codes before learning to wire. Understanding the basic wiring terminology and identifying the common types of wires and cables will help you when investigating wiring problems. It will also help you when you want to choose the correct wires for your electrical projects. The following are the basic electrical wiring elements you need to understand:

a) Wire Size

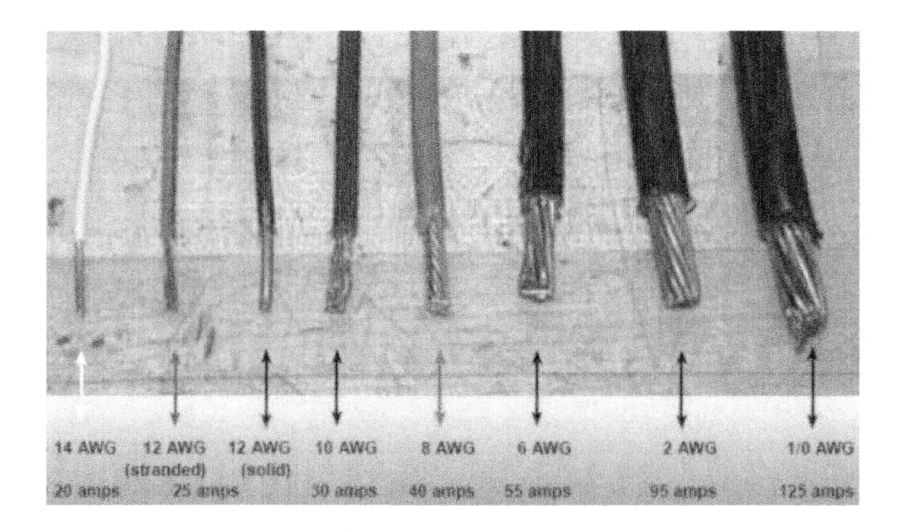

14 AWG	12 AWG (stranded)	12 AWG (solid)	10 AWG	8 AWG	6 AWG	2 AWG	1/0 AWG
20 amps	25 amps		30 amps	40 amps	55 amps	95 amps	125 amps

learn.sonicelectronix.com

It's important to use the correct wire size for any electrical wiring, which is indicated by the diameter of the metal conductor and is established on the American Wire Gauge (AWG) system. A wire's gauge shows the current capacity and the amperage that it can safely carry.

When identifying the correct size of wire, you need to consider the capacity and gauge of the wire and what it can be used for. Wires not matched correctly to the amperage of the circuits can pose a risk of fire and a short circuit.

b) Non-Metallic (NM) Sheathed Cable

electricaltechnology.org

Non-metallic wires are mostly used for interior wiring. The NM cable consists of at least three wires wrapped inside a flexible sheathing or plastic jacket. It is mainly used for internal circuits such as appliances, light fixtures, switches, and outlets. You need to know the correct type for your electrical projects.

c) Electrical Wire Color Coding

ELECTRICAL WIRING COLOR CODES (NEC & IEC) - 1 & 3 PHASE (AC)

www.electricaltechnology.org

PHASE SUPPLY	WIRE & CABLE	NEC - US / CANADA (120, 208 & 240V)	NEC - US / CANADA (277 & 480 V)	IEC - UK & EU	CHINA & RUSSIA (Old)	AUS & NZ	JAPAN	INDIA, PAK & SA
3-PHASE	LINE 1 "L1"							
	LINE 2 "L2"							
	LINE 3 "L3"							
COMMON	NEUTRAL "N"							
	GROUND / EARTH "PG" or "PE"		Or					
1-PHASE	LINE "L"							
	NEUTRAL "N"							

electricaltechnology.org

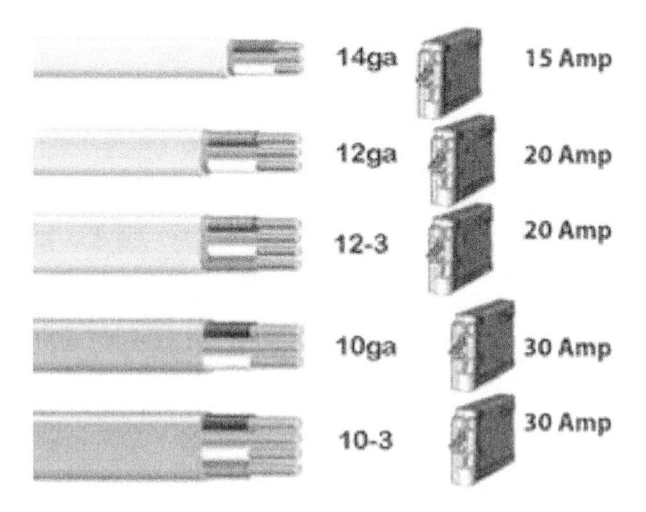

Cable	Gauge	Breaker
	14ga	15 Amp
	12ga	20 Amp
	12-3	20 Amp
	10ga	30 Amp
	10-3	30 Amp

pinterest.com

You will find color-coding on the individual conduction wires and the outer sheath of a bundled electrical cable. Understanding the color code will help you know what each wiring is used for and also helps to sustain consistency in an electrical system. The cable color shows the amperage of the cable and the wire sizes inside the cable. For example, the yellow NM cable is for the 20 amperage circuits, while the white cable is used for 15 amperage circuits.

The coloring on the individual conducting wires does not reveal the rating or size but instead shows the standard use of the wire. For example, white wires indicate they are used in the neutral conductors, and the black and red wires indicate

30

they carry a current, sometimes known as "hot" wires. Wires that are green or copper are used as ground wires.

d) Electrical Wires Labels

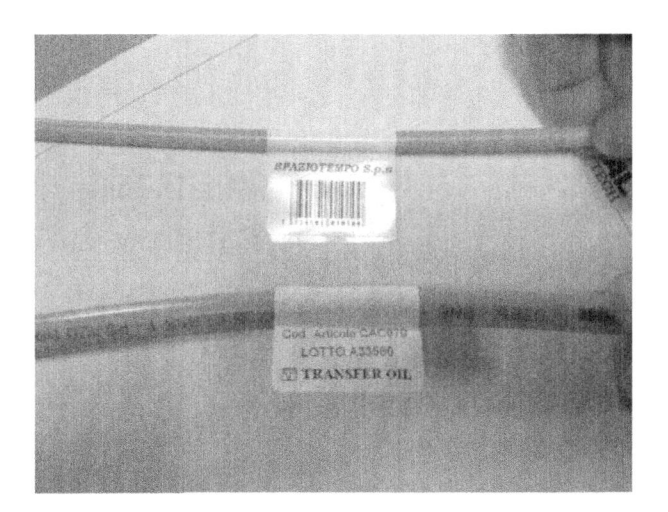

penglaipacking.com

Electrical cables and wires have markings printed or stamped on their outer sheath or insulation. The markings give information on the insulation, the number of wires inside the cable, the characteristics, unique ratings, and the size of the wire. The labels on the wires and cables will help you choose the correct wires for your projects.

With that in mind, let's take a look at some critical wiring safety codes.

Chapter 3: Electrical Wiring Safety Codes and Preparation for Both Indoors and Outdoors Wiring

Electrical codes are enforced to protect you in your home. They are general guidelines that apply to all new installations and provide a clear guide of what electrical inspectors look for. Check with your local electrical inspector on the codes required in your area to ensure your home is safe. Electrical safety at the swimming pool, spas, and hot tubs should be of great importance to you, the homeowner, to keep your family safe.

The following are the electrical code requirements in specific rooms in your house:

1. Bathroom Electrical Codes

Each bathroom needs an exhaust fan, a circuit for lighting, and possibly a blower-heater-light combination. Therefore bathrooms need to be fitted with a 20 amperage circuit, which is different from the lighting circuit, to provide electricity to an outlet that feeds items like dryers, razors, and curling irons.

To protect the user while in the bathroom, the outlet circuit should be connected to an installed ground fault circuit interrupter (GFCI). It is important to do so because it disconnects and trips the circuit power if it senses a short circuit is about to happen or if it takes a different path to the ground that could be right through your body.

Because bathrooms are usually wet, switches need to be grounded to give any stray voltage a path to the ground instead of passing through you. You don't want to get an electric shock when you touch a switch as you are getting out of the bathroom.

For ample lighting in the bathroom, you can install at least one light fixture mounted on the ceiling. This is most likely in addition to the strip lighting. The heater or exhaust fan lights should be installed a reasonable distance away from the shower, hot tub, or bathtub.

You can add extra circuits as you deem fit to accommodate the load in the appliance that you plan to add in the bathroom.

2. Kitchen

Every appliance in the kitchen with a motor should have its own circuit. The major appliances used in the kitchen include the dishwasher, garbage disposal, refrigerator, and microwave. The electrical code requires installing a minimum of two receptacle circuits in the space above the countertop.

An oven or electric range should be wired to a dedicated circuit with a voltage of 240.

3. Bed Rooms, Dining Room, and Living Room

The code requires that these rooms have a wall switch fixed beside the entry door so that you can light the room as you enter. It can control an outlet connected to a desk lamp, a wall, or ceiling light. The ceiling fixture, in particular, should not be controlled by a chain-type light but by a wall switch. The wall receptacles should be 12 feet apart.

On the other hand, the dining room requires a separate 20 amperage circuit for one outlet used for an entertainment center, microwave, or window air conditioner.

4. Stairways

All the steps of the stairway should be properly lit. A three-way switch is the most appropriate- where you fix one at the top and another at the bottom of the stairs. If there is a turning in the stairway, you may require additional lighting to light the area adequately.

5. Hallways

The hallways can be very long and will need adequate lighting to prevent casting any shadows while walking. Three-way switches are required at each end of the hallway. If you have many doors along your hallway, for example, one or two bedrooms, then you will need an additional four-way switch to the circuit at the door of each room.

6. Closets

Globe-covered fixtures are the best to have in your closet controlled by a wall switch. That is because exposed bulb fixtures, like the pull-chain fixtures, can be very dangerous when they get hot, especially when they come in contact with clothing or combustible materials stored in the closet.

7. Laundry Room

The dryer and washer need to have their own 20 amperage receptacle. For an electric dryer, a separate circuit with a voltage of 240 should be installed.

8. **Attached Garage**

There should be at least one switch that controls the lighting inside your garage. For convenience between the doors, a three-way switch should be installed. This is in addition to any other lighting in your garage. Garages usually need a separate circuit, usually a GFCI outlet. Check with your local code to be sure about this, and when in doubt, install a GFCI. Any outlets outside the garage need to be installed with either a GFCI breaker or GFCI outlet.

Following the electrical codes is for your safety and should not be ignored when wiring both indoors and outdoors of your home.

Safety Precautions When Working on a Wiring Project

It's imperative to be extra cautious when working with electricity. Safety should not be compromised. The following are some basic safety guidelines that you can follow to protect yourself when wiring your home:

1. Avoid water when working with electric wires. Do not try to repair any electrical equipment or do any wiring when your

hands are wet. Water increases the conductivity of an electric current.

2. Don't use equipment whose insulation is damaged. Also, don't work with equipment that has broken plugs or frayed cords.

3. Turn off the mains before working on any receptacle in your home. It might be a good idea to put up a sign at the service panel that indicates no one should put ON the main box. This is to prevent anyone from turning it on by accident.

4. Use tools that are insulated. E.g., make sure to wear insulated goggles and rubber gloves when working on any electrical project such as a branch circuit or any other electrical circuit.

5. Unguarded electrical equipment and exposed energized parts can become energized without warning causing electrical hazards. Usually, such equipment has warning signs that read "Shock Risk." Be observant of such signs and carefully follow the guidelines given by the electrical code in your country.

6. Never attempt to repair energized/electrified equipment with 'live' electricity. As a rule, always check and make sure that it is de-energized by testing it. You can do this by using a

tester on all the wires, the metallic box that covers the mains and any other hanging wire.

7. Never use a steel or aluminum ladder; instead, use a wooden or fiberglass ladder. With the former, there is the danger of an electrical surge that can ground you and pass a current pass through your body.

8. Know and understand the wire code of your respective country.

9. Check the GFCI's in your home at least once a month. GFCI's are usually installed to prevent electrical shocks. It quickly disconnects when the current is too high, or a short circuit occurs.

Planning For Your Projects

Planning your wiring projects will help you complete them not only safely but also successfully. The following are steps you can take to plan your wiring project:

1. You need to examine the amperage rating of the electrical service in your main service panel. Also, examine the size of the circuit breaker panel to help you decide if a service upgrade is required.

2. Check with the National Electrical Code, and find out the electrical codes permitted in your home, such as the amount of power and the number of circuits for your rooms. Your local electrical inspector can advise you which wiring regulations apply to the job you want to do.

3. Prepare to have your work inspected by your local electrical inspector. Carefully follow the guidelines for quality work that is safe for everyone in the home.

4. Evaluate the electrical loads because any new circuit will increase the load in your electrical service. Ensure that the total load of the current wiring and the new circuits you intend to add don't surpass the service capacity.

5. Draw a wiring diagram and get a permit. This will help you plan to organize your work.

Chapter 4: Common DIY Indoor Wiring Projects

After understanding the basics of electrical wiring, you can now start your projects. The following is a step-by-step guide on common DIY indoor wiring projects.

1. How to Rewire a Lamp

If your lamp is not illuminating as it should, then the following are probably faulty: the light socket, plug, brass tab, switch, a power outlet, or a faulty cord.

The first step is to troubleshoot the problem. Check out each of the faults and find out which one is causing the problem. For this guide, we shall tackle how to rewire a lamp that has a faulty cord. A faulty cord could occur because it is damaged or worn out and has become brittle. If that is the issue, then you need to remove it and replace it with a new one. This is a project for a beginner and will cost around $15 and will take 2 hours to complete.

Materials Required

- Electrical wiring
- Electrical tape

Equipment

- Screwdrivers
- Wire stripper
- Utility knife
- Pliers
- Clean towels

Procedure

a) Unplug the lamp

Before doing any repairs, unplug the lamp. Below is an overview diagram for rewiring a lamp.

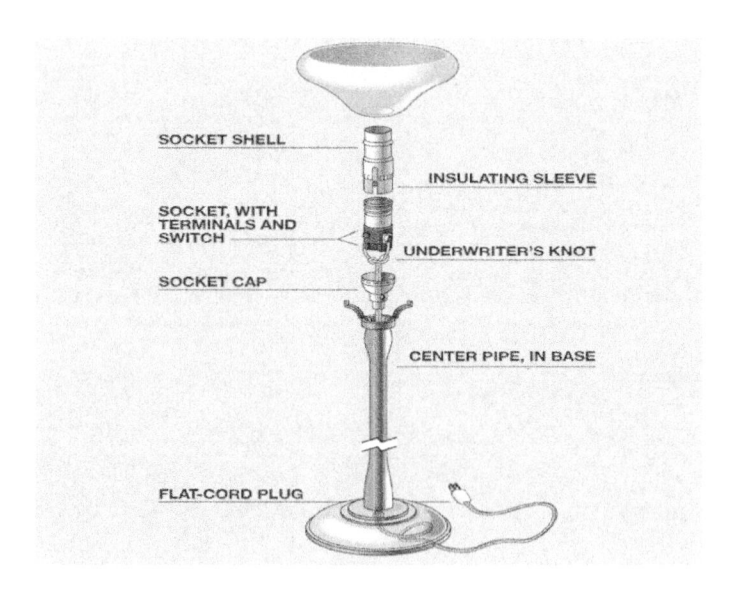

https://www.thisoldhouse.com/

b) Prepare the Work Area

Clear off the surface area that you will be working on and ensure you have enough lighting. Lay the towels on your working surface to protect the lamp, and prevent it from rolling. Have your tools nearby for easy access.

c) Remove the Lampshade and Bulb

Lift the lampshade off by using your hand to turn it counterclockwise to unscrew the finial from the top and then remove the light bulb.

d) Remove the Harp

The harp is the metal part that holds the lampshade, which should be removed gently by pushing the two ends together and at the same time pulling straight upward.

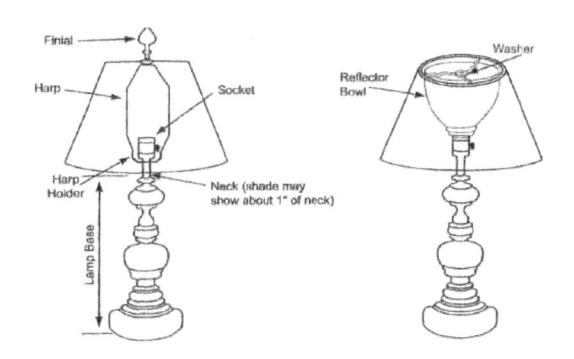

ballarddesigns.com

e) Remove the Protective Base

Most lamps have bases at the bottom that protect the stand on which they are placed, such as a table. Carefully remove the base from the bottom of the lamp.

f) Loosen the Socket

There's a screw that holds the socket in place at the top of the lamp. Loosen the screw and turn the socket counterclockwise and then leave it in place. Don't remove the socket just yet.

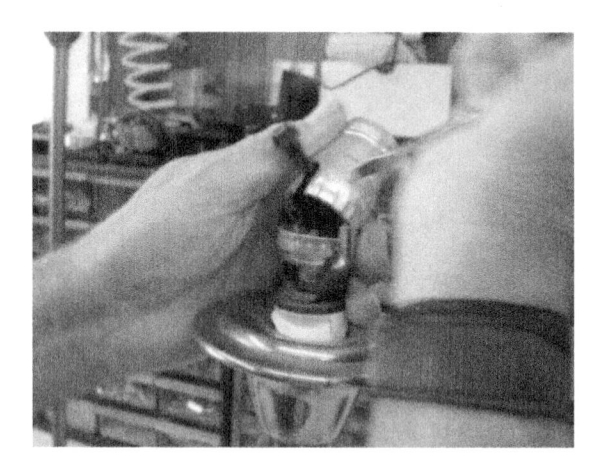

ballarddesigns.com

g) Pull the Wire Out of the Lamp

Cut off the electrical cord at the bottom of the lamp, and leave an extra wire about 2 inches long. Gently pull out the socket and the wire that is attached.

h) Remove the Socket from the Shell

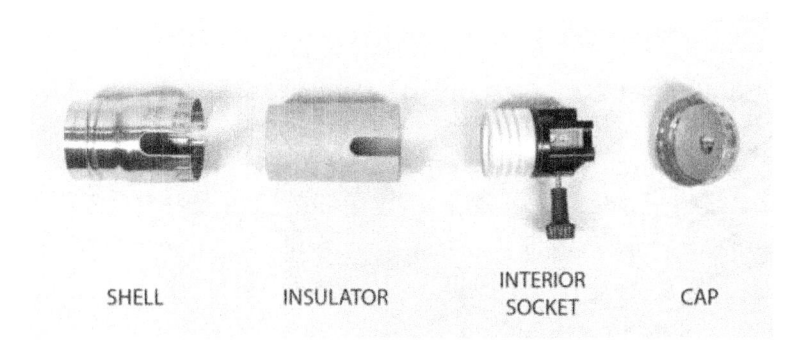

SHELL   INSULATOR   INTERIOR SOCKET   CAP

instructables.com

Using a flathead screwdriver, snap open the exterior metal socket shell to reveal the inner socket. Take out the socket shell, separating it from the socket.

i) Fix the New Wire Inside

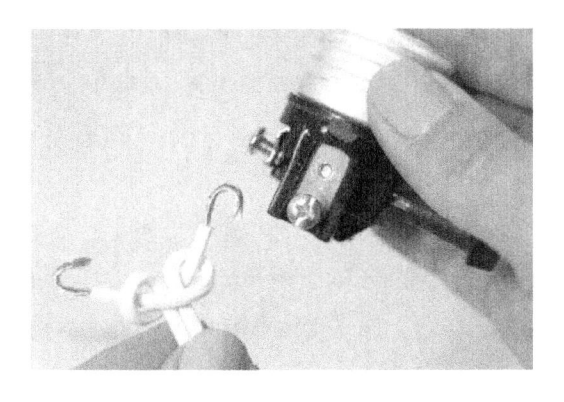

instructables.com

45

Push the electrical cord smoothly through the center of the lamp, leading with the exposed part. When the cord has come out the other end, extending about six inches of wire, tie it into an underwriter's knot. That secures the cord so that it is firmly fixed. You may cut off the excess wire.

j) Attach the Wires to the Socket

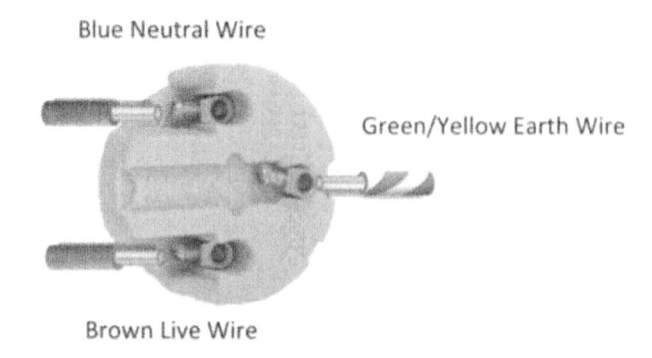

lampholder.net

Using a wire stripper, strip the wires to expose the ends, which you will attach to the terminals of the new socket. Use the screwdriver to screw the wires firmly and securely to the terminals.

Please note you have to fix the correct wire to its respective terminal. You do this by matching the right colors on the socket and the terminals. Attach the neutral wire to the silver terminal and the hot wire to the brass terminal.

If the cord is clear, the silver wire is neutral, and the copper-colored wire is hot. If, on the other hand, you cannot see the wires because the cord is black, brown, or white, then the wire has a smooth surface which means it is a hot wire. The other one, which is ribbed, is neutral.

k) Reassemble the Lamp and Socket

homeguides.sfgate.com

Fix back the socket shell to the socket, and then screw the socket to the lamp. Any excess cord that you have should be pulled out from the base of the lamp. Put back the harp, and place back the protective base at the bottom of the lamp. If need be, glue the protective base.

2. How to Replace a Ceiling Light Fixture

A ceiling light fixture can be replaced because it is worn out or to improve on the décor. A new one can change the ambiance of your home by giving you a new look and feel. Because you have a basic understanding of how electrical circuits work, this is a good wiring job for a beginner.

Materials

- Wire connectors (wire nuts)
- New ceiling light fixture
- Electrical tape (if required)

Equipment

- Non-contact circuit tester
- Screwdriver

Procedure

a) Turn Off the Power

Turn off the wall power controlling the light fixture. Also, turn off the power from the main service panel, as someone else could turn on the switch without your knowledge.

b) Remove the Light Fixture

thespruce.com

How you remove the fixture will depend on the type of fixture that you have. You may have to unscrew the glass shade from the fixture base, unhook mounted clips, or loosen the tiny screws holding the shade up.

After removing the ceiling fixture shade, unscrew the mounted screws to separate the ceiling box from the fixture base.

c) Test for Power, then disconnect the Wires

diynetwork.com

When you separate the fixture base from the ceiling box, test if the power is still flowing using a non-touch circuit tester and continue to unscrew the wire connectors and detach the light fixture from the circuit wires.

If the fixture has a copper grounding wire fixed to the mounting strap on the box, disconnect it and put the light fixture away.

Pull out the old mounting strap connected to the ceiling box because the new fixture comes with its strap.

d) Prepare the New Ceiling Fixture

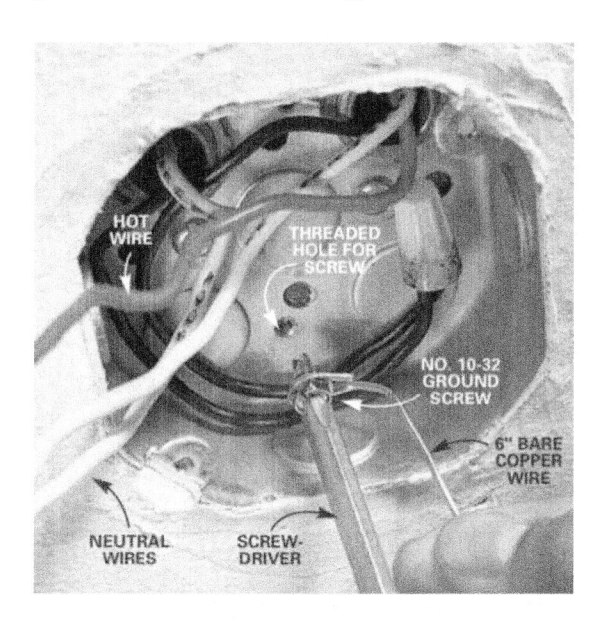

familyhandyman.com

Remove the new ceiling fixture from its box, gently remove the glass shade, and safely place it on the side. Remove the hardware and put it on the side. Check the wires on the fixture base. It will have a bare copper or green ground wire, a white neutral wire, and a black hot wire.

If the light fixture has more than one lamp socket, the white and black wires may not yet be connected. If that is the case, use a wire connecter to join the white wires, and do the same with the black wires.

It's, however, important to always read the instructions to understand how the light fixture will be mounted to the ceiling box. This will largely depend on the weight and size of the light fixture. It may be a simple case of screwing the light fixture base directly to the ceiling box. Another style may require that the mounting strap be connected to the ceiling box, and then the fixture base is screwed to the mounting strap.

For much heavier fixtures, a tube with a threaded mounting is screwed into the hole on the mounting strap. After which, the fixture base is threaded over the tube, and with a screw-on knob, it is firmly secured.

e) Install the Mounting Strap

If your fixture has a mounting strap, you will see several tiny threaded screw holes in it. Some are used to connect the strap to the ceiling box, and others are used to support the light fixture base. You'll also find a larger threaded hole in the center of the strap used if the light fixture is upheld by a threaded mounting tube typically screwed into the strap.

To know the screw holes that will be used to hold the light fixture up, position the strap so that it's adjacent to the light fixture base. Using a screwdriver, attach the mounting strap to the ceiling box.

For heavier light fixtures such as chandeliers, you will have to screw the threaded mounting rod into the center opening of the strap.

f) Inspect the Circuit Wires

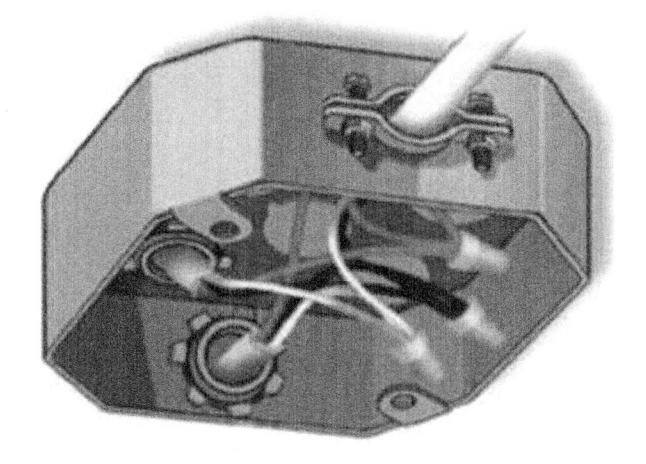

dfarq.homeip.net

Usually, the circuit wires that you earlier disconnected match the new light fixture. However, if the wiring in your house is old, the color coding may be unclear, or the insulation on the wires may be worn out or cracked. If required, use electrical tape to wrap around the old wires.

g) Connect the Ground Wires

amazon.com

Always remember that your light fixture's ground lead needs to have a metal pathway to the circuit grounding wire. It's very dangerous installing a ceiling fixture without the ground pathway.

If your ceiling box is plastic, using a wire connector, connect the circuit ground wire directly to the fixture's ground lead. If the ceiling metal box is metal, you have to connect the light fixture and the box to the circuit ground wire. The most common method of doing this is by looping the circuit ground wire around the green ground screw on the metal box or mounting strap, attaching the ground wire's free end to the fixture's ground lead.

On the other hand, if you find that the circuit ground wire is attached to the metal box, you can attach the mounting strap to the light fixture.

3. How to Install an Outlet Receptacle

Installing an outlet receptacle can be very easy to do when all it involves is replacing the current receptacle. It becomes more difficult to run a circuit from the main electrical box or when an existing circuit needs to be extended. However, for this job, I'll illustrate how to replace the receptacle when the service panel is installed and the NM cables have been passed through the wall cavities. You will learn how to install the standard 120-volt receptacles, which normally come in amperage ratings of 15 or 20. Remember to buy a receptacle that resembles exactly the one you want to replace and has the same amperage. Never install a 20 amperage receptacle on a 15 amperage circuit. However, a 15 amperage receptacle can be installed on a 20 amperage circuit.

As a homeowner, attempting to replace a receptacle can be dangerous if cables have to be run to the new outlet location and if the outlets require a new circuit or extension. It's an easy job to do, but any work that involves the main electrical box can be dangerous if you don't have the experience and expertise for this kind of work.

You can easily identify a 20 amperage circuit as it uses a 12-gauge wire and has a yellow sheath. A 15 amperage circuit has a 14-gauge wire and typically has a white sheath. Besides, the circuit breaker on a 20 amperage circuit is indicated by a stamped mark "20". Also, a 15 amperage circuit has a breaker with a marking showing "15".

The reasons why you may want to replace your receptacle might be because the plastic casing is developing chips or cracks, or the prongs are not being gripped properly over the appliance cords.

This job is excellent for a beginner because it only involves replacing the receptacle when the service panel and circuit wiring are in place.

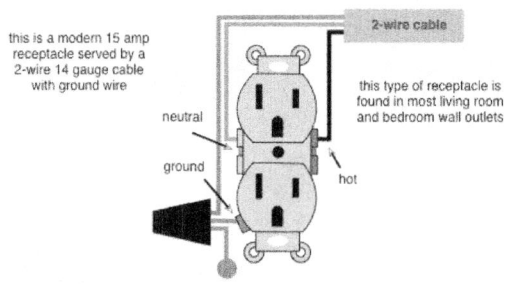

this is a modern 15 amp receptacle served by a 2-wire 14 gauge cable with ground wire

2-wire cable

this type of receptacle is found in most living room and bedroom wall outlets

neutral
ground
hot

-Polarized/Grounded Receptacle
-Hot and Neutral are Separate
-Ground Included

www.do-it-yourself-help.com

pinterest.com

Materials

- 15 amperage or 20 amperage receptacle

Equipment

- Wire strippers
- Needle-nose pliers
- Screwdrivers
- Non-contact voltage tester

Method

a) Turn Off the Power

Shut off the power from the service panel that leads it to the receptacle circuit. You can do this by simply switching off the respective circuit breaker.

b) Test for Power

Insert the tip of your non-contact voltage tester into all the slots of the receptacle to check for power, which should show there's no voltage. At all times, when working on an electrical project, ensure your tester is properly working so that it can give you the correct indication.

c) Open the Outlet

publicism.info

Remove the cover plate by unscrewing the center of the outlet faceplate. Again, test for power by inserting the voltage tester into the spaces next to the receptacle's body touching all the wires inside the electrical box. In both cases, the tester should show there's no voltage.

Remove the mounting screws that hold the receptacle strap to the electrical box, and carefully pull the receptacle out of the box by holding it by its ears, one at the top and the other at the bottom.

When you open the outlet, you will see three wires, each with its respective color attached to the receptacle. There's the hot wire which carries the live current and is attached to the brass-colored screw terminal. There's another white wire normally connected to the silver-colored screw terminal. The bare copper wire, which is sometimes green, is the ground wire. You will also find the pigtail that links the grounding circuit wires to the metal electrical box.

Some receptacles will have only one neutral wire and one hot wire connected to the receptacle. Yet others may consist of two white wires and two hot wires connected to the opposite sides of the outlet. The wiring will largely depend on how the earlier electrician chose to wire the circuit.

d) Confirm the Amperage of the Receptacle

It's essential to verify the correct amperage for the new receptacle. Remember that a 15 amperage receptacle can be safely connected to either the 20-amp or 15-amp circuit. Also, the circuit must have the wiring that relates to the amperage rating. A 20-amp needs a 12-gauge wire, and a 15-amp requires a 14-gauge wire. If, however, you have come across a disparity in the wiring, for example, a 14-gauge wire is fed by a 20 amperage circuit, then do not go ahead with the wiring as it could be an extremely dangerous situation. Call a professional electrician to check it out and fix it for you. But if you find consistency in the receptacle, circuit wires, and the circuit breaker, then you may go ahead and fix the new receptacle.

e) Disconnect the Receptacle Wires

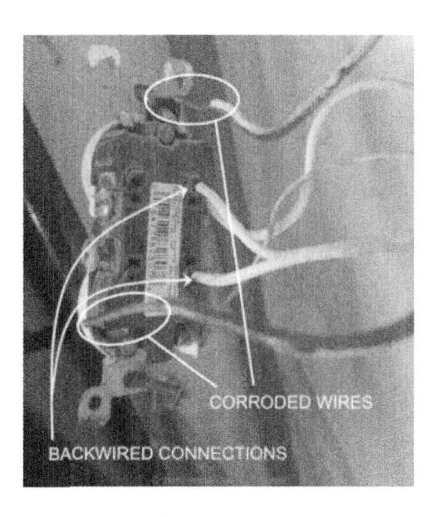

inspectapedia.com

If your receptacle has back-wire connections, insert a flat screwdriver or small nail to release the slot next to each wire. The wire connection will loosen and is set free from the receptacle body. If your receptacle has screw terminals, simply unscrew the screws and separate the wire loops from the screws.

f) Fix the New Receptacle

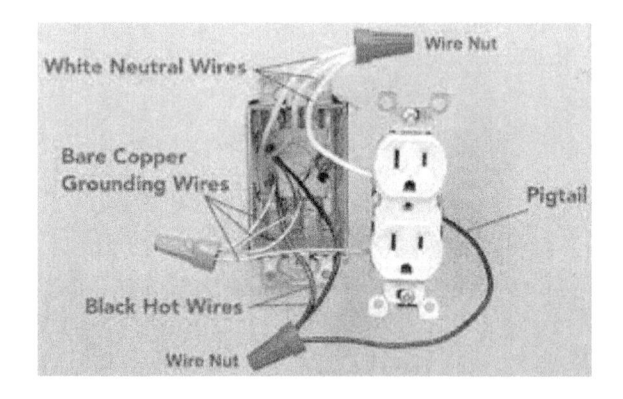

inspectapedia.com

At this point, you are ready to connect your new receptacle. Bend the end of the green insulated or bare copper wire into a C-shaped loop in a clockwise direction, and attach it to the green screw terminal on the receptacle and firmly tighten it.

Do the same with the neutral circuit wire by forming a C-loop at the end of the wire and then attaching it to the silver-colored screw terminal on the receptacle. Screw it firmly in a clockwise direction. Never connect more than one wire to a single terminal.

Please note that some receptacles are manufactured so that the straight ends of the wires have to be inserted into slots next to the screw terminals on the side of the receptacle.

If the old receptacle had a back-wired connection, do not fit it using the back-wire method unless they are the kind that can be firmly secured with a screw. Instead, use wire strippers to trim the ends of each wire and then strip close to ¾ inch of insulation from the wire. Bend the wire into a C-shaped loop and attach it to the screw terminal on the side.

Finally, attach the black wire, also known as the hot wire, to the brass-colored screw terminal, using the same technique you used on the other two types of wires. Again, do not attach the single terminals with more than one wire.

g) Mount the Receptacle and Turn on the Power

As you place the receptacle into the box, tuck in the wires neatly. Firmly screw the receptacle to the box. Install the faceplate onto the new receptacle.

Put on the power to the circuit by switching the circuit breaker. Test the receptacle to check if it is working properly.

There are other variations of the receptacles, mainly the split receptacle and the GFCI receptacle. Each has been explained below.

- **Split Receptacles**

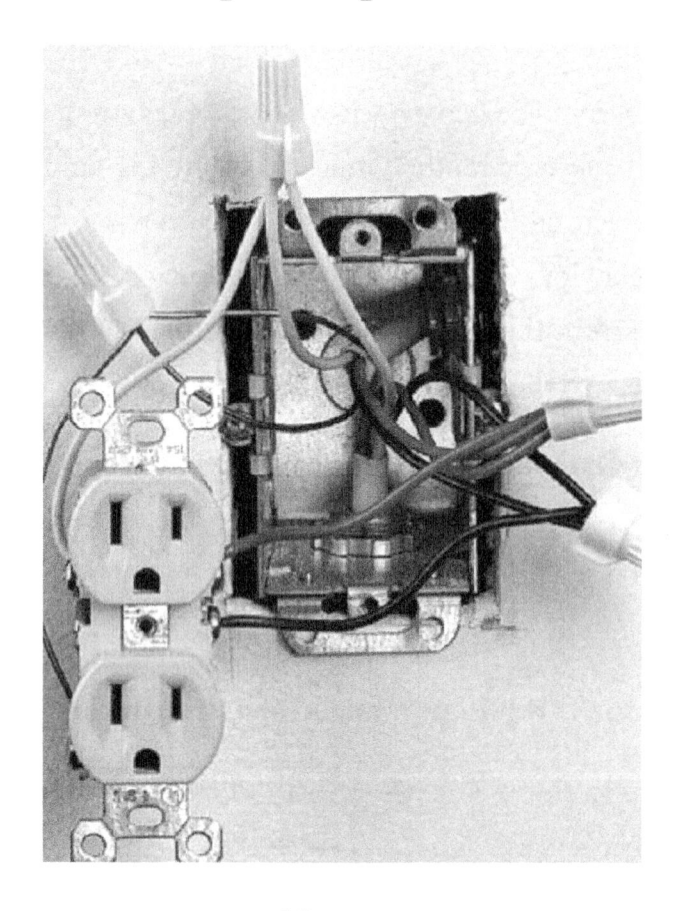

bhg.com

These types of receptacles are not common. The top and bottom halves operate independently and are fed onto different circuits. You can find them in the kitchen countertop outlets.

There's absolutely no electrical pathway between the two halves because the brass attached to the tab along the receptacle side is broken off. When replacing the old receptacle with a new one, check the tabs, and if they have been severed, then break off the tab on the new receptacle before installing it.

- **GFCI Receptacles**

If you understood how the wires were connected in the old receptacle, it would not be hard to replace a GFCI receptacle. The GFCI receptacle has two pairs of neutral and hot wires, and each pair has to be connected to their specific terminal screws. The pair of cables entering the box from the power source will be attached to the neutral and hot screw terminals significantly marked "LINE." The other pair of wires that run to the other receptacles or fixtures should be connected to their respective terminal screws and have the mark "LOAD" on them.

Chapter 5: Outdoor Wiring Projects

There are outdoor fixtures that will require you to carry out some repairs, replacement, or installations at one time or another. These are simple projects that are not difficult and can easily be done by a beginner. The following are DIY outdoor projects that you can handle at your home:

1. How to Replace an Outdoor Light Fixture

ebay.com

Exterior lights are a great way to revamp the look of your front patio. They come in various shapes, sizes, and designs and are a great way to make your patio more attractive and can be a safety precaution. As with any other electrical light fixtures, they have key factors that are common in most.

Your outdoor lights typically have three wires: the ground, which is usually bare copper or green in color, black or red, which are the hot wires, and lastly, the white or gray, which is the neutral wire. Once you understand this, then it's easy to connect the wiring of your new lights. Always connect ground to ground, white to white, and black to black.

It's important to turn off the power from the main circuit breaker before working on any electrical project. Turning off the light from the switch is not good enough because the current will still be flowing to the circuit.

Supplies Required

- Outdoor light fixture with mounting hardware
- Wire connectors
- Wire snips, if necessary
- Screwdriver or power drill
- Clear silicone-based caulk, optional
- Electrical tape
- Level
- Caulk gun

- Light bulb, if it does not come with the light fixture

a) Remove the Outdoor Light

diynetwork.com

Disconnect the power at your fuse box or the main service panel, and do not reconnect until you finish your wiring project. Ensure your working area is dry before you begin your job, and then remove the light fixture from the wall. Unscrew the screws using a screwdriver. Remove the screws while holding the light fixture firmly, and lift it off from the wall. Still holding the fixture, untwist the wire connectors and the wire ends and disconnect them.

b) **Replace the Mounting Bracket**

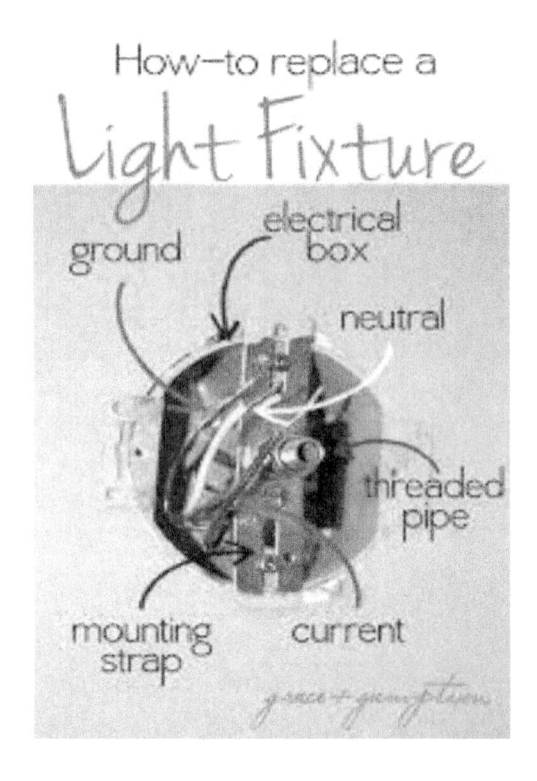

pinterest.com

aconcordcarpenter.com

New light fixtures come with their own mounting hardware, which will be used to replace the old one. Don't use the old mounting bracket because the hole orientation and size of screws vary with different manufacturers. Use the level to ensure the crossbar is level and leave the ground bolt loose.

c) Wire the Outdoor Fixture

Read the manufacturer's instructions carefully and connect the wires of the new light fixture to the junction box on the wall. Start by wrapping the ground wire twice around the threaded ground bolt near the head and tightening it to anchor it firmly. Afterward, connect the wires according to their color; connect white to white, black to black, and ground to ground. Use your hands to twist the ends of the wires together in a clockwise direction.

You need close to an inch of exposed wire to twist the ends together. Therefore, if they are not long enough, use wire snips to trim the top plastic casing away from the wire. Connect the wire ends with the plastic wire connectors or electrical tape. Ensure you have screwed the wire connectors tightly so that they do not come apart.

You can also wrap some electrical tape around the connector's base where the wires meet to waterproof it.

Finally, tuck all the wires into the junction box, making sure none are sticking out.

d) Install the New Light Fixture

bhg.com

Using the hardware provided, attach the new fixture to the mounting bracket. Screw any lockup knobs onto the related screws and tighten to secure them firmly. If the gap between your fixture and the wall is more than 3/16 of an inch, then apply clear silicone-based caulk to seal the gap so that water does not enter inside. A gap is allowed but should not be more than 3/16 inches.

Seal the sides and top of the fixture for any water that gets inside to drain at the bottom. However, if the gap is bigger than 3/16 inches, then correct the error and fix the light fixture properly. Insert a bulb, and turn the power on from the main circuit breaker.

2. How to Wire an Outdoor Time Switch

It's possible to confuse a wire time switch with a timer switch-a device that essentially turns off a device such as a vent or light fixture after a fixed time has been set. A time switch, on the other hand, performs a different function. A time switch basically keeps track of the time of day and turns off and only at times the user desires.

Time switches are mostly used for outdoor lighting, water heater re-circulation pumps, outdoor pond pumps, swimming pool pumps, and any other device that needs to be turned on and off at specific times of the day.

How a Timer Switch Works

alamy.com

There are analog and digital time switches. The analog time switch, which is becoming less popular, has a rotating mechanism that completes one revolution every 24 hours. It is still used for 20 or 40 amperage circuits, like those serving hot tub heating units or swimming pools.

These switches have an additional two or more "on" and "off" switches that open and close the current flow, depending on how the user sets it.

ebay.it

The most common time switches are digital, which have an inbuilt battery to operate. They also have an inbuilt clock that keeps track of time. Digital switch timers can be programmed to turn the current flow off and on many times during the day. They can also be programmed to provide different "on" and "off" cycles on different days within the week. They are typically used on standard 120 volts household circuits.

Below, we shall look at how to wire each type of switch.

Supplies and Tools needed

- Screwdrivers

- Time switch

- Wire strippers or Combination tool

- Wire connectors or wire nuts

- Pigtail wires as required

This is a beginner project, and it shows you how to make basic wire connections for time switches whose switch box and circuit cables have already been installed. Adding a circuit or running cables may require the assistance of a professional electrician before the switches are connected.

- **Wiring a Mechanical Time Switch**

line.17qq.com

Start by switching off the circuit connected to the time switch.

a) Connect the Ground Wire

Begin wiring the ground wires. Take one end of the grounding pigtail wire and connect it to the green ground screw on the time switch. Afterward, using a wire connector (wire nut), join the other end of the pigtail to the outgoing and incoming wires.

Tuck in the ground wires safely inside the switch box, making sure they do not touch the terminal connections. Bend the wires tactfully so that they do not touch the connection points.

b) Connect the Neutral Wire

The next step is to connect the time switch to the neutral wires. Cut 8 inches long of the white insulated wire, which is the pigtail, and strip it up to ½ inches from each end. Insert one end of the pigtail into the screw with the neutral terminal inside the switch and tighten the screw.

Take the other end of the pigtail, join it to the outgoing and incoming white circuit wires, and connect them with a wire nut (wire connector). Tuck the extra wire into the top of the switch box.

Some time switches come with two separate neutral screw terminals, one for the outgoing and the other for the incoming neutral wires. If this is the case, join each circuit neutral wire one of the available neutral screw terminals.

c) Complete the LINE Connection

The connections for the hot wire in a mechanical timer switch include both the LINE and LOAD. The LINE connection is where the incoming hot wire from the power source is connected. The LOAD connection transfers power outward from the switch to the device or appliance.

Strip ½ inches of insulation from the black wire on the cable delivering power from the source or the incoming cable, and insert the end of this wire into the terminal that has a screw marked 'LINE.' Tighten the screw firmly, and then bend the extra wire into the bottom of the box.

d) Finalize on the LOAD Connection

Strip ½ inch of insulation from the black wire in the cable carrying power to the device or appliance, also recognized as the outgoing cable. Take this end and insert it into the terminal with the screw marked LOAD, and then tighten it well. As always, tuck the extra wire into the bottom of the box.

e) Install the Flash Shield

Time switches have wire terminal flash shields installed in them for your own good. They act as shields from a flash that could happen when a hot wire comes into contact with a ground or neutral wire. This shield must always be in place for safety purposes. It is held in place by a plastic tab. You can identify the shield by the reference markings on it.

f) Set The Time

Set the correct time on the switch, and then set the "ON" and "OFF" cycle as you want it. Don't forget to carefully follow the directions from the manual when setting the time.

- **Wiring a Digital Time Switch**

line.17qq.com

Some digital time switches have screw terminals to which the circuit wires are joined. Others have wire leads that join to the circuit wires with wire connectors. There are particularly three wire leads; blue LOAD leads, a black LINE lead, and a green ground lead. Normally, digital time switches do not have neutral wire connections.

Start by switching off the circuit that moves power to the switch box.

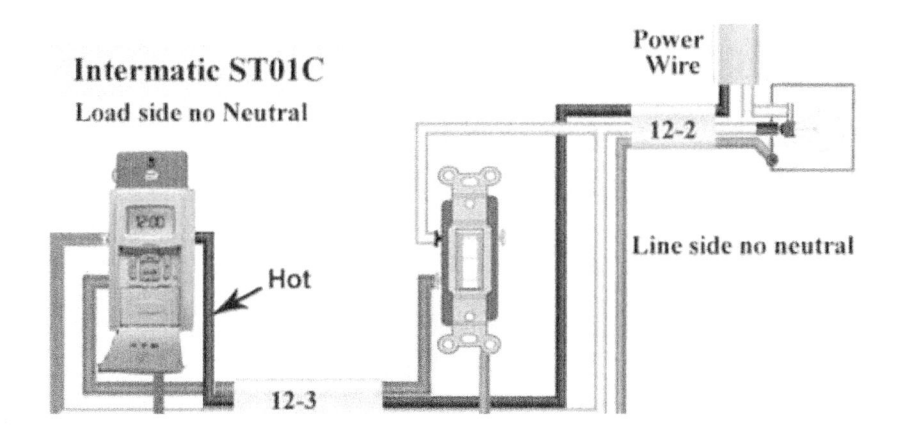

Intermatic ST01C
Load side no Neutral

Power Wire
12-2
Line side no neutral
Hot
12-3

waterheatertimer.org

a) Connect the Ground Wires

With a wire connector, connect the circuit ground wires and the green grounding wire on the switch together. If the switch does not have a lead but instead has a grounding screw, connect it to the circuit grounding wire using a grounding pigtail.

b) Connect the LINE Wires

Using a wire connector, connect the LINE or black wire lead to the hot wire switch from the major power source. If the switch does not use wire leads and instead uses the screw terminals, connect the feed circuit wire to the screw.

c) Connect the LOAD Wire

Connect to the circuit hot wire that leads to the device or appliance with the blue wire lead or the LOAD on the switch.

d) Complete the Installation

Safely tuck the wires into the box and push the switch into the wall box and attach the mounting bracket to the box. Fix the cover plate on top, and then program the switch as per the directions from the manufacturer.

3. How to Add an Outdoor Outlet

You have probably wanted to plug something outside to carry out some work in your backyard or any other outside job, and there was no outside plug. An outdoor outlet is essential when you want to put up decorations during the holiday. Or you may simply just want to listen to your favorite music on the patio, but there's no outdoor outlet to play your record player.

Running an extension cord from inside your house can create tripping hazards, increasing your recipe for electrical shocks or fires. The solution is to install an outdoor outlet. You simply have to tap into an interior circuit to provide power to your outdoor outlet.

Below is a step-by-step guide on how to install a new outdoor outlet.

Supplies Needed

- Hammer
- Wire stripper/cutter
- Wire coat hanger
- Stud finder
- File
- Drill/driver - cordless
- 4-in-1 screwdriver
- 1-inch drill bit

- Electrical tape
- Non-contact voltage tester

Materials Required

- Cable clamps
- Exterior electrical box
- Electrical cable
- GFCI outlet
- Silicone caulk
- Weatherproof box cover
- Wire connectors

a) Select and Mark the Outlet Location

Your new outlet should be in the same stud cavity as your existing indoor outlet. Turn off the circuit breaker that carries a current to the outlet. Take a non-contact voltage tester and ensure the power is off. Unscrew and pull the outlet out of its electrical box. Double-check if the power is off by holding the voltage tester over the terminals.

b) Adjust the Wires

The next step is to unscrew the wires from the outlet. As you remove the wires, check the junction box and make sure it is large enough to hold an extra set of wires. This is because a box overstuffed with wires is a fire hazard.

c) Drill through the Exterior Wall

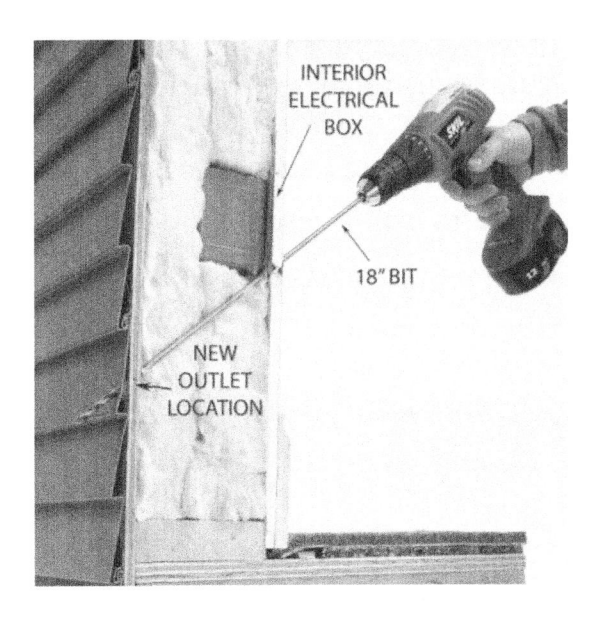

familyhandyman.com

Use a stud sensor to find out which side of the electrical box the stud is on. Place an 18-inches long by ¼ long drill bit along the electrical box's outside on the side away from the stud. Squeeze the bit between the drywall and the box. Drill through the wall and also through the siding to mark the selected location for your new outlet. Tilt the drill a little downward so that the outlet location is lower. Afterward, go outside and drill a ¾ inches hole.

You can also decide to move the location of the exterior junction box, either straight down or up, while maintaining the same stud cavity, and mark the new position of the box hole on the siding. Drill a hole that is one inch over the tinier hole or the mark on the siding to create room for the cable.

If drilling through brick, use a hammer drill with a masonry drill bit. Continue to drill a series of holes that are small in diameter, all around the marked hole. Using a hammer and chisel, knock out the center.

d) Run Cable From Other Power Sources You Have Identified

If you do not have a convenient interior outlet, you will have to look for other electrical circuits to tap power from, such as:

- *Tap From Your Basement*

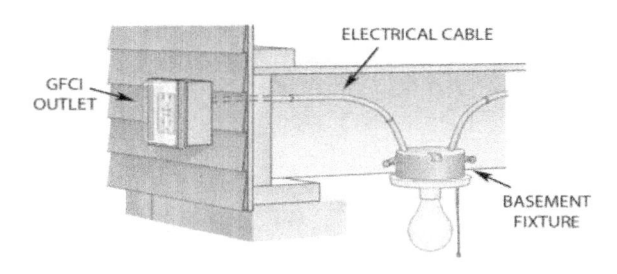

familyhandyman.com

If you have an incomplete basement, you can tap into the junction box in the basement and pass the cable out via the rim joist. This is much easier than tapping into an outlet that's on the main floor. In addition, it gives you the option of putting your new outlet anywhere you wish and not just opposite an interior receptacle.

All you have to do is drill a hole through the rim joist and siding, and then run the cable from the light fixture in the basement to your outlet location.

- *Tap Power from an Existing Exterior Outlet*

Use a service ell to wrap the conduit around the corners. However, do not run it in from of the doors in your home.

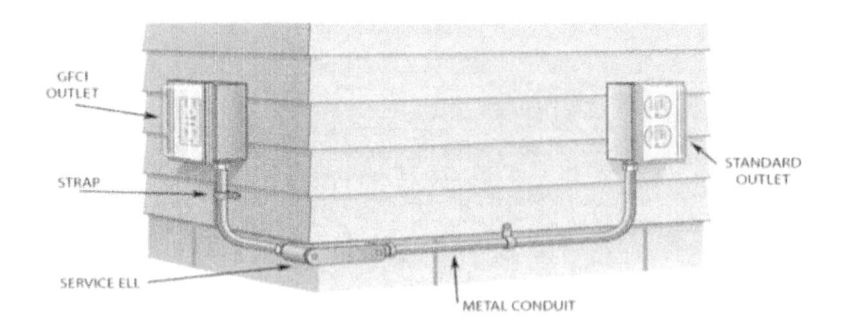

familyhandyman.com

e) Run the Cable between the Outlets

familyhandyman.com

Use a wire gauge similar to the one used inside your interior outlet and connect the cable from the interior box to the exterior hole. Hit the box with a screwdriver to remove the knockout. Strip close to two feet of the sheath off the end of the cable and cut out two of the three wires. Attach the remaining wire to the end of the sheathing using tape to form a loop. Pass the loop through the knockout and into the wall cavity.

Form a hook by bending the end of the coat hanger wire. Insert it through the hole outside, and hold the wire loop in the wall, pulling it back through the hole. Ensure you pull through at least 12 inches of cable, meaning you will have plenty to work with.

f) Replace the Electrical Box

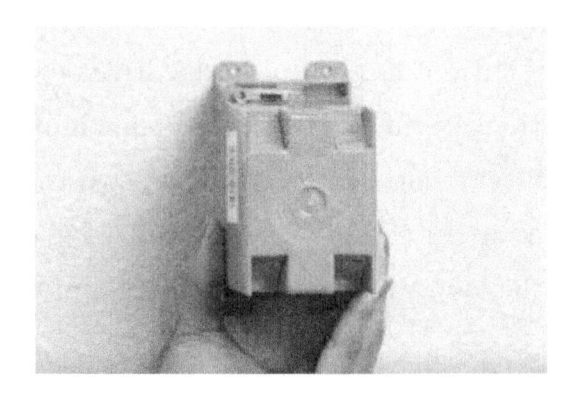

thespruce.com

If your current electrical box is not big enough to hold more wires, you will need to replace it. To remove the box, cut out the nails holding the box in place. Preferably replace the box with a plastic one because they have wings that flip up and connect to the back of the plaster or drywall. Hold this box over the opening on the wall and trace it all around it.

Enlarge the opening using a drywall saw, but be careful not to over-cut it, as you want it to fit snugly. The new cable will be fed from the outlet added into the box before you install it. Using electrical tape, wrap the cable where the sheathing comes into contact with the exposed wires to make it easier for the sheathing to slide into the box.

g) Wire the Interior Outlet

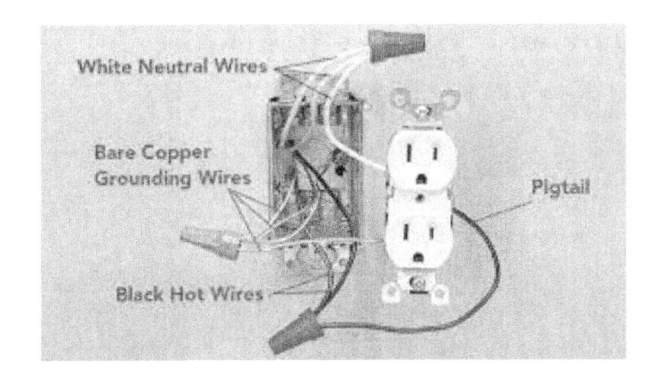

pinterest.com

Cut the cable that's inside the interior box so that there'll be 12 inches sticking out. Expose the wires by removing the sheathing. Cut 6 inches of the wires from the coil—Strip ¾ inches of insulation off the ends. Screw the pigtail wires firmly to the outlet terminals, and then join the wires with wire connectors. Connect the white wires to one of the silver terminals, join the bare copper to the ground screw, green in color, and finally connect the black to either of the brass screws. The wires should be hooked clockwise over the screws to remain in place after tightening the screws.

To wire the interior outlet, connect all the neutral wires, the hot wires, and all the ground wires. Carefully fold the wires inside the box and reattach the outlet and cover plate. If the wall around the box got damaged, you could hide the problem using an oversize cover plate.

h) Mount and Wire the New Outlet

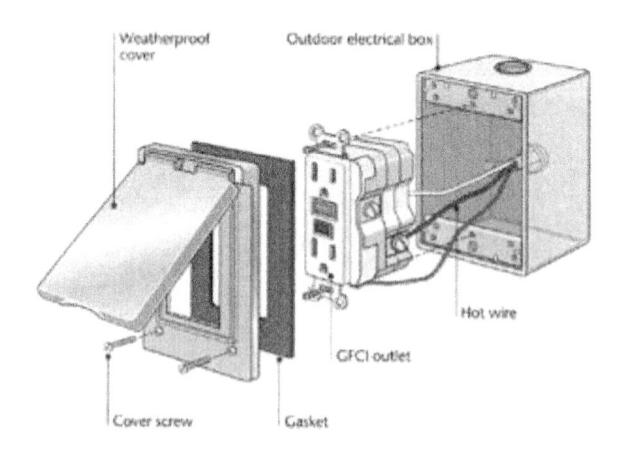

pinterest.com

Begin by attaching a clamp to the box. Feed the cable through the clamp and into the box and caulk around the clamp. The caulk ensures the hole is watertight. Mount the outdoor outlet box to the wall of the house. With the exterior grade fasteners, mount the junction box to the house if the sheathing you have is wood, hardboard, fiber cement, or plywood. Drive the galvanized deck screws through the mounting lugs. For stucco or brick siding, mount the box using masonry anchors. Use hollow wall anchors for vinyl siding over the composition board.

Fix the plugs into the openings at both ends of the box. With a file, scrape a small "weep hole" or notch at the bottom edge of the box. This is done to allow water that gets into the box to drain out. Strip the insulation off the ends of the wire.

Connect the green screw inside the box with the ground wire and also the green screw on the GFCI outlet. Ensure you have identified the white, hot, and line terminals. They will normally be labeled "white," "hot," and "line." Join the white wire to the push-in or silver screw and the black wire to the adjacent push-in hole or brass screw. Snip the ears off the outlet; fold the wires neatly into the box, and fix the outlet in place.

i) Mount the Weatherproof Electrical Outlet Box Cover

finehomebuilding.com

Remove the middle part of the plastic cover base to make it fit over the GFCI outlet. The central part is designed to come out easily by using pliers to twist it. Fix the base on the box, over the outlet, ensuring the hinges are at the top. By doing this, the plastic cover closes properly over the outlet. Using the screws that came with the cover kit, join the base to the box and attach the cover to the base. Carefully push the hinges of the receptacle sideways over the hinges until they click into place. Remove the cord knockouts at the base where the electrical cords run and turn the power on.

4. How to Install Low-Voltage Landscape Lighting

You can place exterior lighting anywhere in your compounds, such as the driveway, walkway, or patio. You could also decide to illuminate the fence, stonewall, trees, steps, and other conspicuous landscape features in your home. The low-voltage landscape lighting project that we will tackle is excellent for beginners and safe enough because the system operates at an electrical voltage of 12.

In this project, you will learn how to install landscape lighting alongside the walkway leading up to the entryway. We will install two fixtures near the fence on either side of the walkway, each with a wattage of 20. There'll also be light fixtures at the base of each of the four green shrubs growing near the house. All the 12 fixtures will be joined together with a 12-gauge cable and powered by a 300-watt transformer.

The following is a step-by-step guide:

Equipment Needed

- Flat Blade Shovel
- Wire Stripper
- Screwdriver
- 12-inch long steel punch
- Small hedge hammer

a) Have an Overview of the Landscape

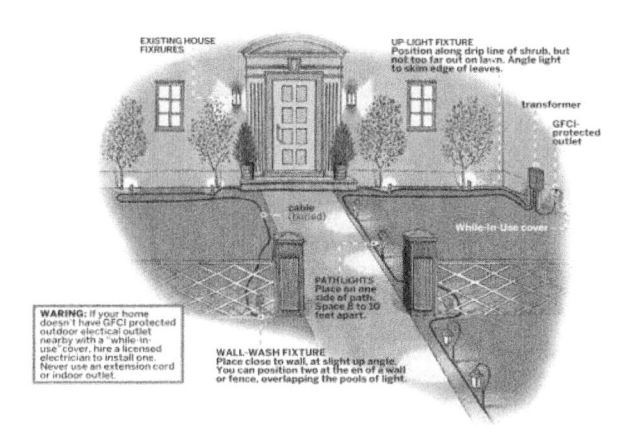

thisoldhouse.com

After creating an overview of how you want your landscape to look, you will need only three components; the fixtures, low-voltage electrical cables, and a transformer. The transformer lowers the 120 voltage current to just 12 volts. The transformer should be plugged into an outdoor electrical outlet that is GFCI protected and fitted with a cover and an oversize plastic box that shuts firmly over the power cord.

The transformer must have the capacity to support the cumulative wattage of the lights within the system. The cable will be buried in a shallow trench between the fixtures. Also, note that the fixtures should be 10 feet away from the transformer.

b) Lay the Components Accordingly

Put the light fixtures onto the ground where they will be installed, generally between 8 and 10 feet apart. Next, lay out the low-voltage cable beside the concrete walkway, following the line of the outdoor light fixtures. Get a 14-gauge cable that can light systems totaling 200 watts or less and a 12-gauge cable for systems that hold more than 200 watts. When you encounter an obstacle such as a shrub or fence, string the cable around or under it.

c) Turn Over the Sod

savvygardening.com

After identifying where the light fixtures will be installed, move them so that you can begin digging the trench. With a flat-blade shovel, slide below the top layer of grass, 12 inches away from the edge of the walkway.

Next, separate the grass from the soil by lifting the handle then proceed to fold over the scalped portion of sod.

Continue doing this throughout your walkway. Scratch a 3 inches deep trench using the corner part of the shovel's blade. This is the trench where you will place the wire. If needed, fix the light fixtures on top of the sod already folded to prevent it from flopping back down.

d) Bury the Electrical Cable

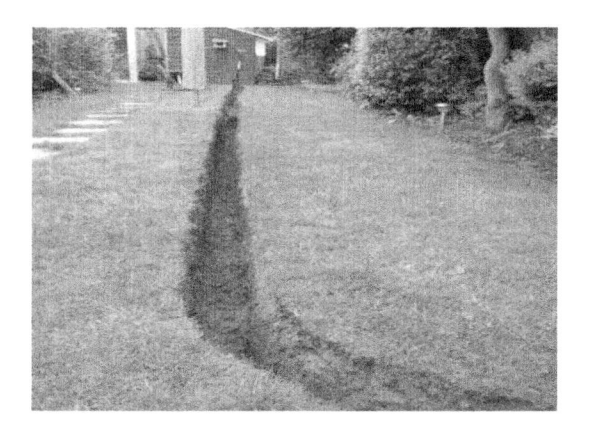

pinterest.com

thisoldhouse.com

Place the cable in the trench and ensure some slackening at the points where the fixtures will be installed. This gives you enough wire cable to fix the light fixtures. Cover the trench smoothly with the soil. Make sure you leave the cable sticking up out of the soil next to each fixture.

Create a slit within the detached sod exactly at the point where your fixture will sit then proceed to fold back the sod over the soil and as you do that, place the cable for each of the fixtures above the grass. It's important that you do not bury the cable further than 3 inches down; otherwise, you will find it difficult to connect the light fixture.

e) Plug in The Transformer

in-sider.com

Run the cable to your outdoor electrical outlet. Use wire strippers to cut the cable then proceed to strip off the rubber insulation by half inch. Slither in the stripped wires to the bottom of the transformer and under the two terminal screws. Tighten the screws to grip the cable firmly in place. Next to the outlet, drive a wooden stake into the ground, and screw it to the transformer. Alternatively, you can mount it directly on the wall of the house. Lift the cover on the outlet and plug in the transformer.

f) Prepare Holes for the Fixtures

Put the light fixtures to their original position, making sure that they are equally spaced. Start with the first fixture by positioning it as close as possible to the walkway's edge with no part hovering over it. If the fixture extends into the walkway, people will occasionally bump into and probably trip over it. Using a long steel punch or large screwdriver, make a hole in the ground, where you will fix the stake, onto which the light fixture will be inserted. Never attempt to use a hammer to drive the fixture into the ground. Also, never place a light within 10 feet of a fountain, spa, or pool.

g) Make the Electrical Connections

prettyhandygirl.com

Glide the two connector halves dangling from the underside of the light fixture over the cable that's protruding from the sod and firmly push them towards each until you hear a click.

The cable is then pierced with the sharp prongs right into the connectors, to make contact with the wires that are located deep inside.

Plug in the transformer, after which the fixture ought to light up to confirm that your connection is fine. If it doesn't, unsnap and then pop back the connector or check the bulb. If none of the bulbs light up, you may likely have a faulty outdoor electrical outlet or transformer.

h) Install the Light Fixtures

Infix the light fixture to the designated metal ground stake. Use both hands to push the fixture as well as its stake into the ground until the top of your stake is on the same level as the ground. Look closely to make sure the fixture is not tilted to one side. Tuck the connector and the cable under the sod and stuff them into the soil, 2 inches deep. Install the other fixtures using the same method.

i) Replace the Sod

pinterest.com

After ensuring all the light fixtures are installed and working properly, level out the sod around the fixtures. Press the sod down firmly, and soak the area with water. When a bulb burns out, replace it immediately so that it will not shorten the lives of the other bulbs.

Chapter 6: Tips for Easier Electrical Wiring in Your Home

You now know how to handle both indoor and outdoor projects that you can do as a beginner. Wouldn't it also be great to have some tips to make your electrical wiring in your home easier? Let's delve into some helpful tips:

1. Uncoil cable without kinks: It becomes a lot easier to pull cables with plastic sheaths through holes when you first straighten the cable out.

2. Neat tack in the wires inside the electrical box: When you neatly fold the wires inside the box, it becomes easier to identify the wires and gives you a lot of room for the switches.

3. Ensure no-snag on your fish tape connections: You do not want to have your tape get stuck on something inside the wall as you pull it back when working your fish tape to its destination. Always fish and push the wire as required without creating a mess by getting caught on an obstruction.

4. Check the full wall cavity: After locating the wall cavity between the two studs, vertically run the stud finder to check if the wall cavity could be having obstacles such as abandoned and blocking headers. You do not want to find out later as you are working that your wire cannot extend to where you need it.

5. Electrical tools you must have: The two tools you cannot do without if you plan to be doing electrical jobs include the glow rods and the flex bits. Glow rods are easy to spot after you have drilled your hole, especially if you are working in dark areas. On the other hand, Flex bits are great for drilling holes in spaces that are difficult to reach.

6. Push through the extra wire: Always make sure you have at least five to six feet of extra wire to hold up the tension on the hook as you pull through. It becomes a real challenge when you want to grab a wire, and after having hooked it, you don't want to lose it.

7. Identify wires correctly: Save yourself a lot of trouble by clearly understanding the wires. This helps you know which wires to connect and which ones should not be connected.

8. Test wires before starting on an electrical project: This cannot be said enough. Never start any wiring job without first testing if the power is off. You can use a non-contact voltage detector to check all the wires in the electrical box or the area you will be working to ensure they do not have a current running through them.

9. Test GFCI Outlets: Ground circuit interrupters save hundreds of lives each year because they detect any dangerous current flow and instantly shut off the power. However, after 10 years, the sensitivity of your GFCI starts to wear out, and sometimes the test button may not indicate there's anything wrong. Therefore, it's good to test the GFCI to make sure they are working properly.

10. Strip the sheathing from your cable first: Remove the sheathing from the wires before pushing them into the box. It is much easier doing this than stripping the sheath later.

Conclusion

This is an excellent book for you who wants to learn how to DIY wiring projects. These are simple projects explained step-by-step to help you understand clearly from the beginning to the end. In this guide, you get to learn about the electrical system in your house, the critical aspects of electrical wiring that you need to know before starting out any project, and the safety precautions you have to take considering electricity can be a hazardous element that can cause severe injury or fatalities.

The projects have been carefully chosen to give an all-around feel of how most electrical wiring jobs are done for both indoors and outdoors. They give you a good footing or base, onto which you can comfortably advance your knowledge on electrical wiring.

Good luck on this journey!

Printed in Great Britain
by Amazon